THIS
MOMENT
IS FULL OF
WONDERS

Welcome
to the
country
of the
Present
Moment

THIS MOMENT
IS FULL OF WONDERS

THE ZEN CALLIGRAPHY OF
THICH NHAT HANH

CHRONICLE BOOKS

SAN FRANCISCO

First published in the United States of America in 2015 by
Chronicle Books LLC.

First published in the United Kingdom in 2015 by Thames
& Hudson Ltd.

Library of Congress Cataloging-in-Publication Data
available.

ISBN 978-1-4521-5155-7

Manufactured in China

Cover design by Jennifer Tolo Pierce

10 9 8 7 6 5 4 3 2 1

Chronicle Books LLC
680 Second Street
San Francisco, California 94107
www.chroniclebooks.com

Chronicle books and gifts are available at special
quantity discounts to corporations, professional
associations, literacy programs, and other organizations.
For details and discount information, please contact our
corporate/premiums department at corporatesales@
chroniclebooks.com or at 1-800-759-0190.

CONTENTS

Introduction

Breathing in, I calm my body.
Breathing out, I smile.
Dwelling in the present moment,
I know this is a wonderful moment.

Everything we are looking for is right here in the present moment. When you wake up, you have joy when you see that you're alive and that twenty-four brand new hours have been delivered to your doorstep. What a gift. Yet so often we look to the past or the future, and we ignore the wonders that are right in front of us.

Mindfulness is the energy that allows us to stop and be present right here and right now. It allows us to notice what is going on in us and around us. All of my work and all of the calligraphies in this book are essentially just invitations to stop whatever else you are doing, to stop all the thinking, worrying and judging, and just breathe.

The breath is the vehicle to greater mindfulness. It is the tool that makes the present moment accessible. When you breathe in mindfully, you bring your mind home to your body. Whether your body is relaxed, tense, or tired, the first step is noticing that it is relaxed, tense, or tired. That is already insight. That awareness is the beginning of being more peaceful.

When I draw a calligraphy, I do not think. I know that thinking is sometimes productive, but most of our thinking is useless. When I draw, I just enjoy drawing. When you breathe, just enjoy breathing. When you walk, just enjoy walking. When you look at a piece of art, just look. Learning to stop the thinking takes some practice. We're used to thinking each moment of each day.

In the Zen tradition, poetry, art, and meditation always go together. The moment when I take a sheet of paper and begin to draw is not exactly the moment of the calligraphy's creation. Whenever I'm practicing mindful walking, breathing, even while cutting carrots, the art is being created. A work of art is conceived in the depths of your consciousness while you're not thinking about it. The moment when you begin to draw is only the moment when you deliver the baby you have been carrying. When I produce a calligraphy, what I care about is that the work embodies the energies of insight and compassion that I have been cultivating in daily life.

For me, doing calligraphy is itself a practice of meditation. Each session of calligraphy begins with tea. I never write calligraphy without first having a cup of tea. I need the tea to help me stay awake and draw calligraphy well. Tea and meditation have been together for many thousands of years. Long ago, the monks and nuns who practiced sitting meditation found that if you drink tea, then you can stay awake and you don't fall asleep during sitting meditation.

I like to drink tea and I drink a lot of tea, so I have a lot of experience looking deeply into it. If you look deeply into your tea, you can see a cloud. This tea has former lives and in one of its former lives it was a cloud. Not that long ago, it was a cloud floating in the sky, having a good time up there. One day it dispersed and was no longer there. The cloud became rain. The rain became the water for my tea. Then, when I drink the tea and begin to draw, the tea disperses and transforms into the calligraphy.

Of course the cloud and the rain don't really die. There is no dying; there is only transforming and changing. A cloud can become the rain, the snow, or the ice but a cloud can never become nothing. The same is true with everything else, including us human beings. We can never become nothing. We just transform.

When I am making calligraphy, I always mix some tea into my Chinese ink. So, if you look deeply into the calligraphy, you can see the tea inside. If you look more deeply, you will see something else. While doing calligraphy, I practice mindful breathing. I hold the brush and I breathe in for one, two, three seconds. During that time of breathing in, I make about one third of the circle. When I breathe out, I finish the rest of the circle; I take about five seconds to finish it. While I'm breathing in, I'm concentrating on my in-breath. When I'm breathing out, I'm concentrating on my out-breath. Sometimes I smile during the out-breath to relax my body. There's no tension at all when I draw a circle. So when you look at the calligraphy, not only can you see a cloud, and not only can you see the tea, but you can also see my breath.

The hand that draws the calligraphy doesn't act alone. It is connected to my whole body, my mind, and all the cells in my body. I like to invite all my cells to join me in making a circle. These cells don't exist by themselves either. I invite all my ancestors to draw the circle with me, as well as all the people whose lives have touched mine. My whole community is in each calligraphy. Please don't think that these calligraphies are drawn by one person alone. We as a community have drawn this circle together.

A Bell of Mindfulness

When I was a young monk in Vietnam, each village temple had a big bell, like those in older Christian churches in many countries. Whenever the bell was invited to sound, all the villagers would stop what they were doing and pause for a few moments to breathe in and out in mindfulness.

In Plum Village, the community where I live in France, we do the same. Every time we hear the bell, we go back to ourselves and enjoy our breathing. When we breathe in, we say silently, "Listen, listen," and when we breathe out, "This wonderful sound brings me back to my true home."

This is the only moment that is real. To be present and enjoy this moment is our most important task. The sound of the bell is an invitation to use our breath to reunite mind and body and come back home to this present moment.

There are bells of mindfulness around us every day. The sound of a car honking and the ringing of your phone can also be reminders to stop, breathe, and come home. The beautiful sky is there available to you at every moment to look at and enjoy. This beautiful planet and the solid ground beneath your feet are always available to you. The whole world is full of these gentle reminders that help us come back to ourselves. Each of these calligraphies is also a bell of mindfulness, a reminder of the beauty in you and around you. You already have everything you need.

CONSCIOUS

BREATHING

breathe
you are alive

The joy of beginning to meditate is like leaving the busy city and going off to the countryside to sit under a tree. We feel ourselves filled with peace and joy. What a relief! Breathing in, we know we are alive. This is already insight. When we breathe mindfully, we reclaim our territory of body and mind and we encounter life in the present moment. The fact that we are alive is truly a miracle. We could say there is nothing special about it, but when we are deeply aware of being alive in this moment, we see how wonderful it is.

Peace
in myself
Peace in
the world

WALKING

Peace
is
every
step

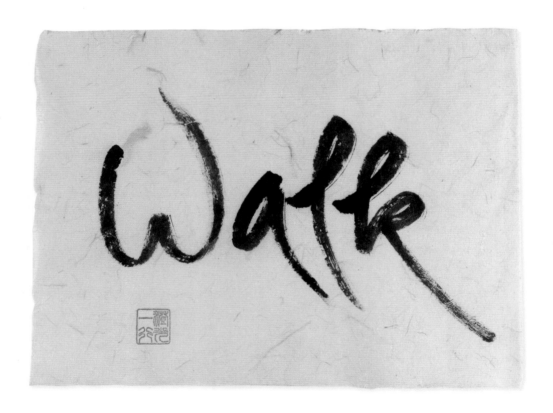

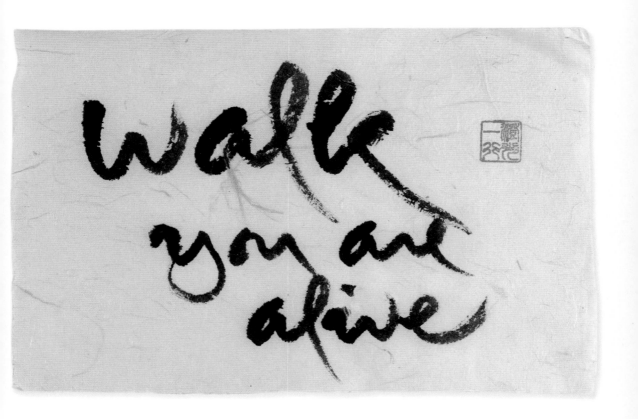

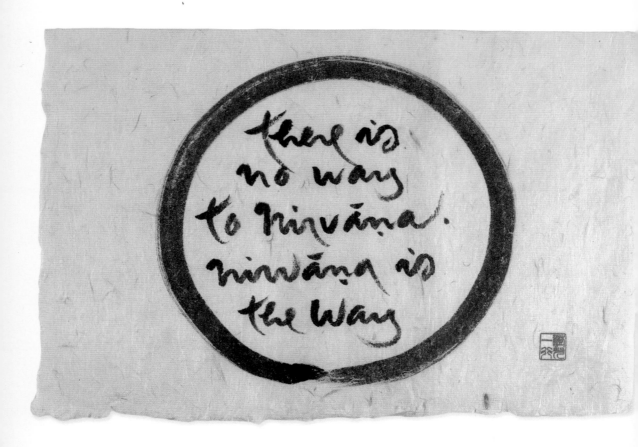

The miracle is not to walk on thin air
or on water. The miracle is to walk
on Earth. The Earth is so beautiful.
We are beautiful also. We can allow
ourselves to walk mindfully, touching
the Earth, our wonderful mother,
with each step. If we want to enter
Heaven on Earth, we need only one
conscious step and one conscious
breath. Why rush? There is no need to
struggle. Enjoy every step you make.
Every step brings you closer to your
true home.

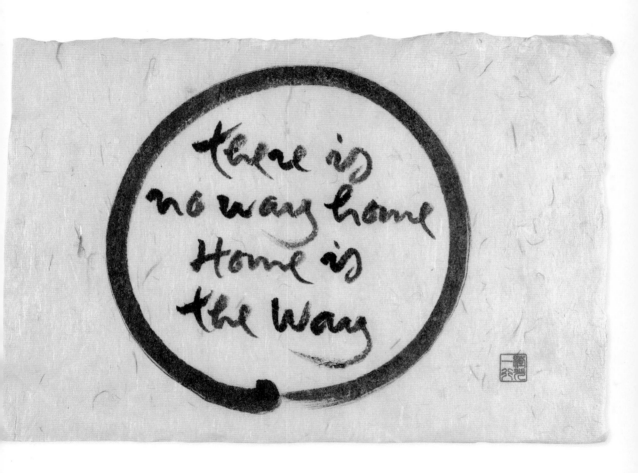

i am
in love
with
mother
Earth

LOOKING

DEEPLY

Be Still and know

Stop
and
be

Stopping brings your body and mind together, back to the here and now. When you stop and sit quietly and become silent within, you become more solid, more concentrated, and clear. Often we tell ourselves, "Don't just sit there, do something!" But when we practice awareness, we discover that the opposite may be more helpful: "Don't just do something, sit there!" We must learn to stop from time to time in order to see clearly. This is not just a reaction; it is a way of life. Humankind's survival depends on our ability to stop rushing.

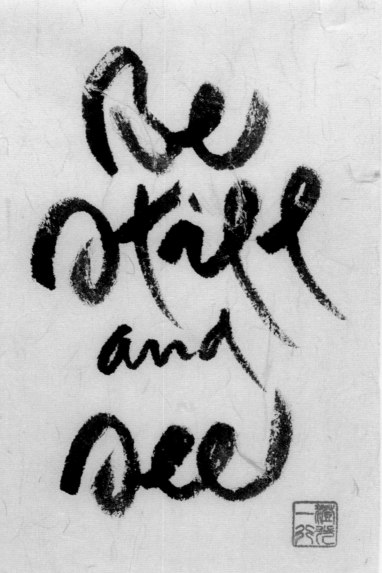

smile to
in yo

the cloud
is tea

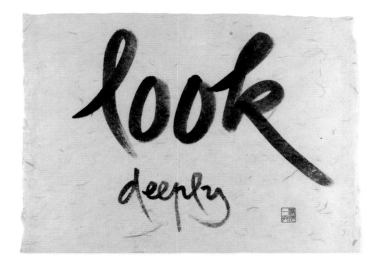

Compassionate listening has one purpose: to help the other person suffer less. Many of us have lost our capacity for listening and using loving speech. So we feel very lonely even with our loved ones. Understanding is the foundation of love. If you cannot understand yourself, you cannot love yourself. If you cannot understand your loved ones, you cannot love them. When communication is cut off, we all suffer. When we recognize our own suffering and that of our loved ones, our compassion grows and we suffer less. Healing can begin.

51

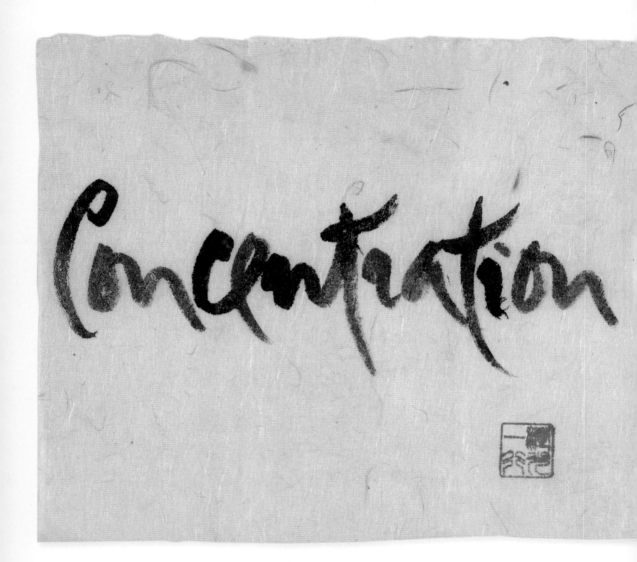

53

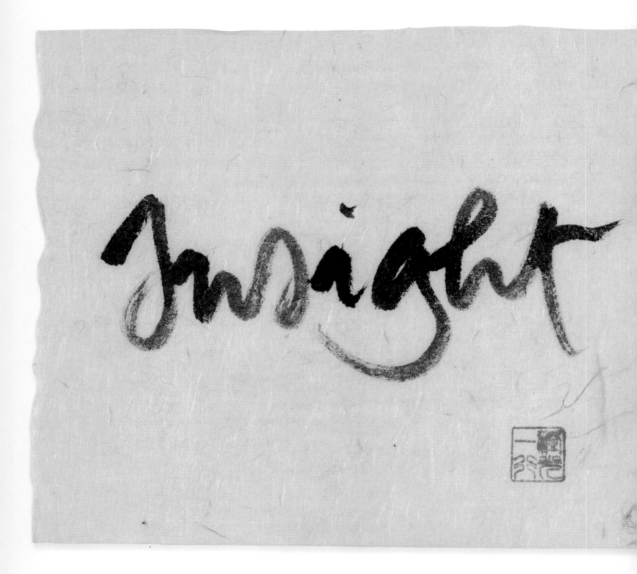

Thanks to our ability to stop, we are able to observe. That is mindfulness. The more deeply we observe, the greater our mental concentration becomes. Stopping and collecting our mind, we naturally become able to see. This is insight. In observing, the mind becomes increasingly still. We do not need to search for anything more.

Revere
the nature

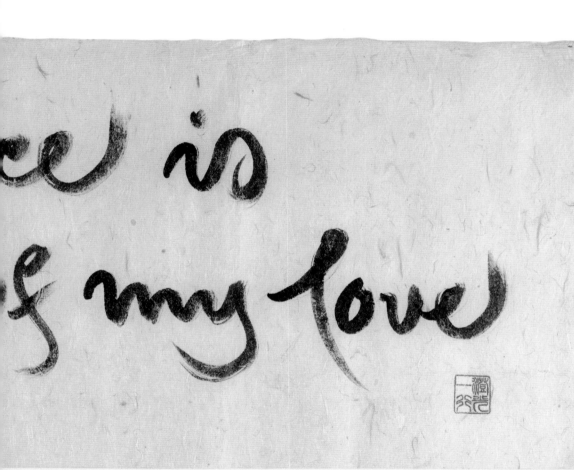

LETTING

GO

Aimlessness is sometimes called
wishlessness and it is one of the
"three doors of liberation." The idea
is that you do not put something
in front of you and run after it,
because everything is already here,
in yourself. There are things we
should be able to leave behind for
joy to be possible. Usually we think
that joy is something out there,
something we have to go and get.
But the obstacles to our happiness
are not primarily outside of us; they
are in us. If we know how to identify
an obstacle and let it go, then joy
naturally comes to us without
our trying to run after it.

the miracle
is to be
alive

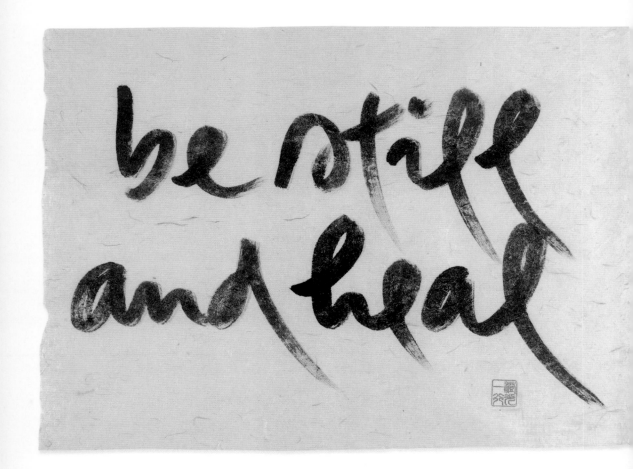

Healing
is
every
Step

Be
free
where
you
are

go
as
a
river

If our hearts are big, we can be like the river. When our hearts are small, our understanding and compassion are limited and we suffer. We can't accept or tolerate others and their shortcomings and we demand that they change. But when our hearts expand, the same things don't make us suffer anymore. We have a lot of understanding and compassion and can embrace others. We accept others as they are, and then they have a chance to transform. So the big question is: how do we help our heart to grow?

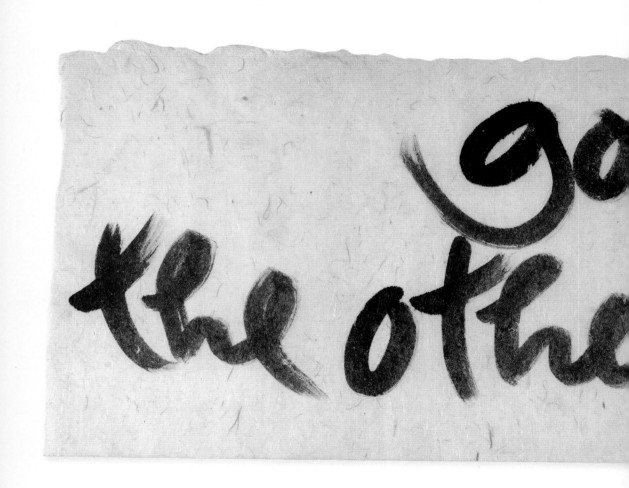

to
phae

BEING

HERE

Present
moment

wonderful
moment

be alive
be the
miracle

While breathing in, enjoy your
in-breath, and you may get the insight
that it's wonderful to be alive. This
kind of insight can arise when you
allow your mind to be entirely with
your breath, without interruption by
thinking or talking. Your in-breath
helps cultivate not only mindfulness,
but also concentration and insight.
Breathing in mindfully, we can get
the insight that being alive is the
greatest of all miracles.

a
cloud
never
dies

this is bea

use that is

93

this is it
be home

Fresh
as a
flower

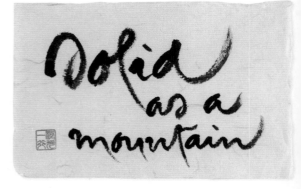

Solid
as a
mountain

Still water
reflecting

Free
as space

Breathing in. Breathing out.
I am blooming as a flower.
I am fresh as the dew.
I am solid as a mountain.
I am firm as the Earth.
I am water reflecting
what is real, what is true.
I feel there is space deep
inside of me. I am free.

the
Pure
Land
is here
and now

the most
beautiful
place of
Heaven
is on
Earth

The seeds of peace and joy are in everyone. Searching for these seeds outside of yourself is like a wave running to search for the water. She will never find it. She has to go home to herself with the strong knowledge that the water is within her. Anyone who maintains awareness in the present moment naturally emanates peace, joy, and happiness, and becomes beautiful. A calm half smile and a loving heart are refreshing, and they allow miracles to unfold.

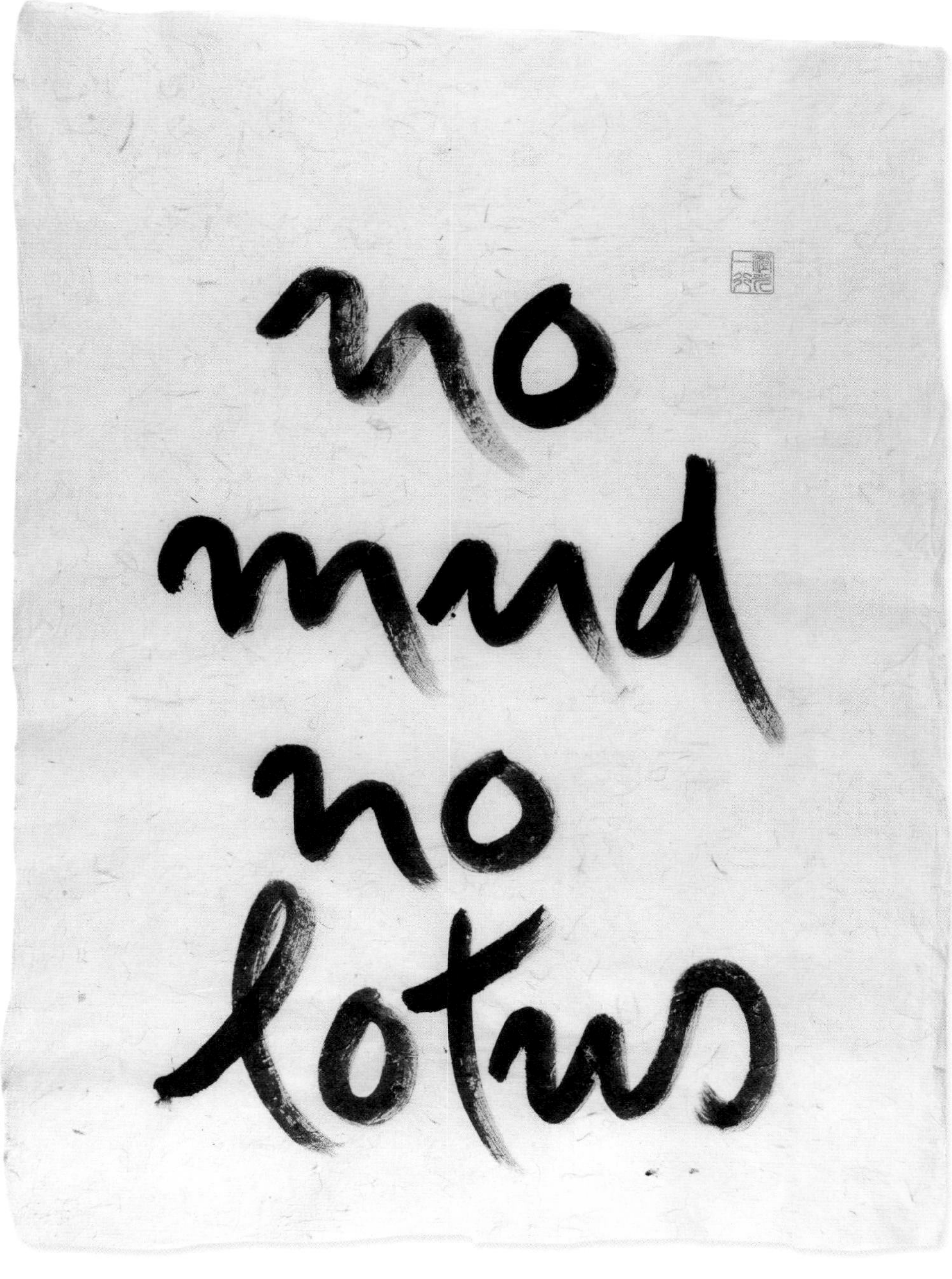
no
mud
no
lotus

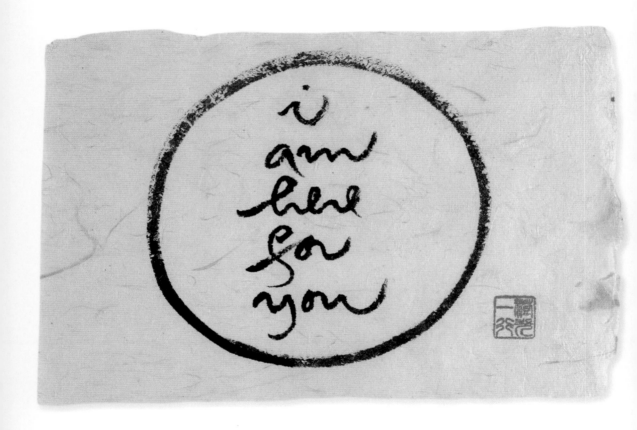

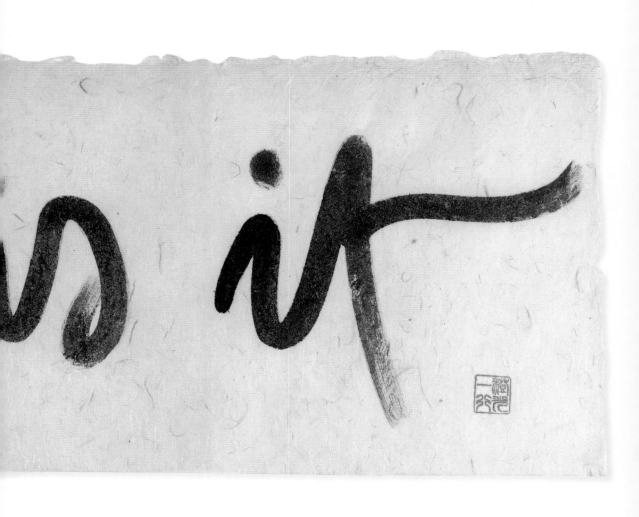

ACKNOWLEDGMENTS

The texts on pp. 17, 27, 37, 47, 57, 67, 77, 87, 97 and 107 are drawn from unpublished dharma talks and extracts from the following titles by Thich Nhat Hanh: *Our Appointment with Life: Discourse on Living Happily in the Present* (1990); *Teachings on Love* (revised edition, 2006); *Happiness: Essential Mindfulness Practices* (2009); and *Breathe, You Are Alive! Sutra on the Full Awareness of Breathing* (20th anniversary edition, 2013), all published by Parallax Press.

The publishers would like to thank Rachel Neumann of Parallax Press (www.parallax.org) and the Buddhist community of Plum Village (www.plumvillage.org).

ABOUT THE AUTHOR

Thich Nhat Hanh is one of the best-known and most revered Zen masters in the world today. A peace and human-rights activist, prolific poet and author, he has written nearly 100 titles, among them the bestselling *Call Me By My True Names*, *You Are Here*, *Peace Is Every Step*, and *Teachings on Love*. His books have sold millions worldwide and have been translated into more than twenty languages. Among his many awards, the most notable are his nomination by Martin Luther King, Jr. for the Nobel Peace Prize in 1967 and the Courage of Conscience award in 1991 for his peace efforts in his native Vietnam.

Photo Eva Yuen, courtesy Plum Village